W9-BSD-789

MAL

Americans All biographies are inspiring life stories about people of all races, creeds, and nationalities who have uniquely contributed to the American way of life. Highlights from each person's story develop his contributions in his special field — whether they be in the arts, industry, human rights, education, science and medicine, or sports.

Specific abilities, character, and accomplishments are emphasized. Often despite great odds, these famous people have attained success in their fields through the good use of ability, determination, and hard work. These fast-moving stories of real people will show the way to better understanding of the ingredients necessary for personal success.

WITHDRA

Milton
Hershey
CHOCOLATE KING

by Mary Malone

illustrated by William Hutchinson

GARRARD PUBLISHING COMPANY
CHAMPAIGN, ILLINOIS

SOMERSET COUNTY LIBRARY
SOMERSET, PA. 15501

Picture Credits:

Hershey Archives. Milton Hershey School, Hershey,
Pennsylvania: p. 20 (both), 26, 34, 43, 53, 59, 70

Hershey Estates: p. 76 (top)

Hershey Foods Corporation: p. 2, 76 (bottom)

DEC (1) 1971

Copyright © 1971 by Mary Malone

All rights reserved. Manufactured in the U.S.A.

Standard Book Number: 8116-4565-7

Library of Congress Catalog Card Number: 74-131020

Contents

1. Pennsylvania Dutch

"I wish I had a penny," Milton Hershey said as he rode to market early one day in September 1864. He was thinking about Felix's Candy Store in Harrisburg, Pennsylvania.

Milton's father, Henry Hershey, stopped whistling and pinched his son's cheek. He was tall and good-looking, with a long, silky beard and brown hair curling under his broad-brimmed hat. "Maybe two pennies, for a boy who's going to be seven years old next week," he declared. He opened a small black purse and took out two bright coins, which he handed to Milton.

"Oh, Father, thank you!" Milton bounced up and down in the wagon. "Hurry up the horses," he said impatiently.

Milton's people were farmers, and every Saturday they went to the city to sell their produce. They got up at dawn to do their chores and load the farm wagon with butter, eggs, and vegetables. By eight o'clock they had traveled over ten miles of backcountry roads on the way to the Horseshoe Pike and Harrisburg.

Mrs. Hershey, slender and neat in her dark dress and little white cap, held the baby, Serena, on her lap. She smiled down at her young son, squeezed between her and his father. "For candy again?"

Milton nodded solemnly. He was dressed in the Pennsylvania Dutch manner, in a dark coat, long trousers reaching to his heavy boots, and a round hat with a wide brim.

When they reached the market, the Hersheys unloaded their farm wagon and arranged the produce. Soon customers began to arrive. Milton helped his parents until there was a lull. Then he tugged at his mother's sleeve. "May I leave now, Mother?"

"For just a little while, Milton. You know that you must mind Serena when she wakes up."

Milton nodded and beckoned to his cousins, Stoner and Rohrer Snavely, whose stand was across the road from the Hersheys'. He showed them his money. Stoner whistled. "Some sour balls for me,

Milton," he said. The boys already knew how Milton would spend his money.

At Felix's, Milton took his time, gazing long at the molasses sticks and licorice before deciding on taffy and sour balls. Then with bulging cheeks, the boys walked slowly back to the market. Milton still had enough candy to last the rest of the day. When he climbed into the wagon for the ride home, sleepy and satisfied, he hoped he'd have more pennies next week. Before dozing off, he had already decided how to spend them—at Felix's.

Milton was asleep on the homeward journey through the quiet Pennsylvania countryside. His people, the Hersheys and the Snavelys, had lived here in the Lebanon Valley for a hundred and fifty years. They had come from Switzerland along with many others for the religious

freedom promised by William Penn. Milton had been born in 1857 in the fieldstone farmhouse built by his great-grandfather, Isaac Hershey.

Farming was the main occupation of these German-speaking settlers who were called "Pennsylvania Dutch." Milton's family and neighbors were Mennonites, a religious group which based its strict beliefs entirely on the Scriptures of the Bible. Mennonites were also called "Plain People" because of their sober dress and way of living. They owned their own farms and kept to themselves, avoiding worldly pleasures like playing cards and attending the theater. Going to market was their chief form of recreation.

The Mennonites tried to avoid the political troubles of the time too. They refused to bear arms in the Civil War.

After the battle of Gettysburg in southern Pennsylvania, a rumor spread that the Confederate army, led by General Robert E. Lee, had won and was marching to Philadelphia. Some Mennonite farmers moved with their families to safer places further north. Others, like Milton's uncles, Abraham and Benjamin Snavely, buried their money and valuables, and remained where they were.

Milton remembered what his uncles had done, and one day he decided to bury *his* treasure—some pennies given to him by Aunt Mattie Snavely. Often he had heard her say, "If you save your pennies, they will grow into dollars." He had dug a small hole under an oak tree behind the house and buried his pennies in a little tin box. Then he had waited for a money tree to sprout. When nothing happened after a week, Milton dug up his pennies. There they were—the same few he had buried. How disappointed he was!

That was a year ago. Milton was older now and knew better. Whenever he had pennies now, he saved them until market day. Then he spent them at Felix's.

He enjoyed his treat even more when he shared it with Stoner and Rohrer. Two pennies—even one—bought enough candy in those days for all of them.

2. Learning His Trade

Milton started school when he was seven, in a little one-room schoolhouse in the village of Derry Church, two miles from home. The schoolmaster was young Elias Hershey, another uncle, who had trouble maintaining order. When he wasn't looking, his twenty pupils did a lot of "scrounging"—shoving each other off the long wooden benches. The smaller and younger ones, who sat on the ends of

the benches, were pushed to the floor most often. All the boys, Milton included, thought that scrounging was great fun.

The school term was short in those days, during the months when there was little farm work to keep the children busy. However, Milton learned a little reading, writing, and arithmetic at the first school he attended.

When Milton was nine, Henry Hershey sold the family farm and bought another near Nine Points in Lancaster County. Here he tried growing fruit trees and evergreen plants, but he did not do very well.

Henry Hershey was ambitious for his son. "Milton must have a good education," he said often. "There are so many new things to learn, so many good books for him to read!"

Still, at the "Old Harmony" School in Nine Points, Milton preferred singing hymns to studying arithmetic and reading. He liked to sing "Shall We Gather at the River?" and then answer heartily with the others, "*Yes*, we'll gather at the river!"

Learning geography lessons was almost as enjoyable, because they, too, were sung.

"Milton Hershey, tell me the capitals of Maine and Massachusetts," the schoolmaster would order. Standing up promptly, Milton would sing out: "Maine: Augusta on the Kennebec River; Maine: Augusta on the Kennebec River. Massachusetts: Boston on the Boston Harbor; Massachusetts: Boston on the Boston Harbor."

Milton repeated the different capitals of the states so many times he knew them all by heart. His favorite geography song was "Pennsylvania: Harrisburg on the Susquehanna." He said those big, mouth-filling names over and over again.

The Hersheys moved several times during Milton's childhood. The Snavely relatives did not approve of Henry Hershey's "flitting" from farm to farm, as the Pennsylvania Dutch called it. He should settle down and stay in one place, they thought. Milton was not happy, either, because each move meant he had to attend a different school, and he couldn't seem to do well in any of them.

When Milton was eleven, a tragic event occurred. His little sister, only five years old, died of scarlet fever. Afterward, his parents centered their hope on him, their only child. As much as he wanted to please his father, Milton never became a

Milton's parents, Henry and Fanny Hershey

good student. Mr. Hershey found it hard to accept this fact, but Mrs. Hershey was more understanding. So was her sister— lively, sharp-tongued Aunt Mattie—who came to live with the family.

Milton did so poorly in his last school that he was asked to leave. Henry Hershey threatened to go to the school and raise a row. "Such treatment of my son!" he stormed. "Why, Milton certainly can learn advanced subjects!"

Mrs. Hershey shook her head. "Milton is fourteen," she said quietly. "He has had enough of books and schools."

Aunt Mattie agreed. "Milton should learn a trade," she declared.

Henry Hershey didn't like that idea, but the two women overruled him. Milton, listening to the argument, was glad when his father at last consented to let him stop school. Next day Mr. Hershey came home and announced, "I've arranged to have you apprenticed to Sam Ernst, the printer. Maybe someday, Milton, you'll be a newspaper editor."

Sam Ernst published a little German-English weekly newspaper in the town of

Gap, not far from the Hersheys' home. He was a farmer and a miller, as well as a printer. Milton, as was usual with apprentices in those days, moved in with his instructor's family. Between setting type and tending the printing press, he did chores on the Ernst farm. As time went on, he preferred the chores to being scolded about his mistakes in setting type. Sam Ernst was very short-tempered. One day when Milton stumbled and upset a tray full of type, the printer shouted at him. "Blockhead! Clumsy oaf!"

A few days later Milton accidentally dropped his tattered straw hat on the rollers of the press. The weekly edition was just coming off, and Sam Ernst was furious. He fired Milton on the spot.

Milton trudged home, relief overcoming his remorse at being so careless. He was

sorry to disappoint his father again, but in his heart Milton knew that he would never be a newspaper editor. Unhappily, though, he wondered if he would ever find the kind of work he liked.

When Milton's father heard what had happened, he was upset. He drove off at once to see the printer.

While Mr. Hershey was gone, Milton's mother and his aunt talked over the latest crisis in Milton's education. By the time Henry Hershey came home, they had the matter settled. "Sam Ernst says you may go back, Milton," he began, but Mrs. Hershey put in decidedly, "No, Henry." Then she continued, "It's plain that Milton doesn't want to be a printer. He should be learning some other trade."

Milton looked up quickly. His spirits rose. He felt better still when Aunt

Mattie said, "I've heard that Royer's wants a boy to learn the confectionery business. Let Milton try that."

Royer's! Lancaster's best confectionery store! Milton's heart beat faster.

Henry Hershey was not impressed by Aunt Mattie's suggestion. "What!" he exclaimed. "A boiler of sugar? A fine occupation for my son!" He kept objecting, until he looked at Milton and saw the interest on the boy's face. Then at last he said, "All right, Milton, go ahead and apply at Royer's." The next day the whole family, including Aunt Mattie, drove to Lancaster.

Royer's Ice Cream Parlor and Garden was known throughout the city for fine candy and delicious ice cream. The prospect of working there delighted Milton. His eyes sparkled as he eagerly sniffed

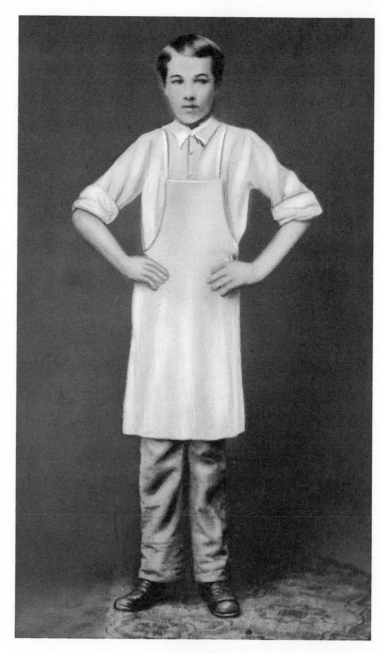

Young Milton Hershey, in his work apron, was glad to be an apprentice at Royer's Ice Cream Parlor and Garden.

the pleasant aroma. "I know I'll like this!" he told Mr. Royer after learning what the apprentice's duties would be. Mr. Royer was pleased by Milton's enthusiasm. "I'll take you on, Milton," he said, "and I'll teach you all I know."

The Hersheys were well satisfied. Mrs. Hershey paid the apprenticeship fee with money saved from the sale of her butter and eggs. Later, the family moved to Lancaster across the street from Royer's, so that Milton could live at home.

Milton was fifteen when he started at Royer's. He was soon helping Mr. Royer with all kinds of jobs—making candy, decorating cakes, roasting nuts, even turning the handle of the ice cream freezer by hand. Making ice cream was hard work, for it took a lot of effort to move the handle of the big churn.

Sometimes Milton even had to mind the customers' horses. "Milt! Out in front!" Mr. Royer would call. Then Milton would hurry out to the street to hold and fondle the head of a waiting horse.

Mr. Royer was pleased by Milton's progress in learning the confectioner's trade. "I never have to explain to Milton more than once," he said.

Milton enjoyed candy making, whether it was taffy, fudge, or "dipped goods"— candies coated with chocolate. Taffy, however, was the mainstay of the confectionery business in those days. Making it required close attention to the stove.

"The temperature is very important," Mr. Royer said. Like all experienced candy makers, he could sense the "crack" of the candy—how to tell when it had reached the exact time to be removed from the heat. Often he watched Milton stirring the taffy. "After it boils, watch it," he warned. "Don't let it thicken. There! It is ready now to be pulled." "Pulling" the taffy meant stretching it from hooks in the candy kitchen until it was thin and chewy.

Although he worked very hard, Milton enjoyed evenings with his friends. The opera house was next door to Royer's, and they often went there. Milton had decided that Mennonite strictness would not govern his life.

One night, sitting in the gallery of the opera house, he began to sniff the smell of burning peanuts. He jumped from his seat and, followed by his friends, rushed to the street. The big blower on Royer's roof showered them with peanut shells. Without hesitating, Milton raced into the store and shut off the blower. Afterward, Milton explained sheepishly, "I was roasting peanuts for peanut fudge." The boys thought this was very funny. Only a short time before, Milton had proudly invited them to watch him make candy.

In 1876 Milton Hershey was nineteen. Four years at Royer's had taught him almost everything about the confectioner's trade, including Mr. Royer's "secrets" of making candy. "I think it's time to go into business for myself," he told his mother and his aunt. "I've saved a little money in the last two years."

"Fine!" Aunt Mattie declared. Milton's mother, too, was pleased by his decision.

"I can give you some money, Milton," Aunt Mattie went on, "enough to get started. And I'll help you to find a good place in Lancaster."

"Not Lancaster," Milton said. "I think I'd have a better chance in a big city like Philadelphia."

A few days later Milton and his aunt went to Philadelphia to look for a suitable shop. At last, on Spring Garden Street, they found a narrow brick house with a store front, a kitchen in the back, and rent low enough for Milton to afford. He took it at once, and shortly afterward, helped by his cousins Stoner and Rohrer, he moved a few pieces of furniture and his new candy-making equipment from Lancaster. Small and poor though his surroundings were, Milton was thrilled and happy. He was in business for himself!

3. M.S. Hershey, Confectioner

At first Milton was all alone in his new business. After a short time, however, his mother and his aunt moved to Philadelphia to be near him. Mrs. Hershey kept house, and Aunt Mattie tended the store while Milton made the candy. Henry Hershey, who was never happy in one place very long, traveled about the country, always seeking, but never finding his fortune. Occasionally, he paid his family a visit.

The first items Milton sold were "penny

candies," and his first customers were the neighborhood children. Sometimes Milton stopped making candy long enough to sell his wares from a pushcart in the Philadelphia streets. During that first summer, in 1876, the Philadelphia Centennial Exposition was held at Fairmount Park, and Milton went there every day with his pushcart. He also passed out business cards he had had printed. These were gaily decorated with pictures of birds and flowers and announced that "M.S. Hershey, Confectioner" sold fine candies, fruits, and nuts and was also a fancy cake baker.

Milton was greatly encouraged when an old family friend from Lancaster came to Philadelphia to help in the business. Big, burly Harry Lebkicher walked in the shop one day and said, "I've come to stay, Milton." Gladly, Milton let Harry keep the accounts and hire a horse and a battered old wagon to deliver the orders.

Now Milton worked longer hours in his kitchen, making candy and dreaming up new ways to make it attractive. He tried using different names and different kinds of wrappings for his taffy. One kind, called "French Secrets," was wrapped in paper with printed rhymes such as:

> *Roses are red, Violets are blue,*
> *Sugar is sweet, And so are you.*

Mrs. Hershey and Aunt Mattie wrapped

the candy in their spare time. Henry Hershey stopped by one day and helped— he thought—by urging Milton to do things in a big way.

"Sell cough drops," he advised. "Don't let the Smith Brothers corner the market." To please him, Milton tried making and selling cough drops for a short time.

Yet with all this help, "M.S. Hershey, Confectioner" was having trouble. Milton began to realize that hard work alone wouldn't keep the business going. Most of his trade was in penny candies. These sold well but did not bring in much money. Stores purchased from him on credit, yet the warehouse where Milton bought sugar refused to give *him* credit. To make matters worse, the price of sugar rose higher and higher. Overwork and worry made Milton ill. He had to stay in bed for

several weeks while Aunt Mattie and
Harry ran the business. The bills continued to pile up.

Aunt Mattie never stopped trying to
make Milton's business a success. She
collected overdue accounts and gave Milton
as much of her own money as she could.
To her brother, Milton's Uncle Abraham,
who owned a big farm near Lancaster,
she wrote, "Please send $200 at once.
Milton needs the money to buy sugar."
Again, later, she wrote, "We need $400 by
the first of the month." She promised her
brother that the money would be returned,
and Milton's uncle responded to these and
several other appeals. Milton struggled on.

One day Harry Lebkicher limped back
to the store, his clothes torn, his hands
scratched. A wheel of the rickety old
wagon Harry used for deliveries had

caught in the trolley car tracks and the whole load had upset.

"What happened to the candies?" Aunt Mattie asked.

Harry managed a grin. "They disappeared, so they did. The whole neighborhood came running—and scooped 'em up!"

Milton shook his head. "I'm afraid it's the last straw!"

Soon Milton had to face the worst. His candy business was a failure. It had cost a great deal of hard work and many hundreds of dollars. Sorrowfully, he had to tell his mother and Aunt Mattie, "We must close."

Milton borrowed his uncle's horses and wagon to move the candy-making equipment back to Lancaster. Then he, his mother, and his aunt returned home. Harry Lebkicher stayed in Philadelphia.

Not long after he left Philadelphia, Milton received a letter from his father. Henry Hershey was in Colorado, having gone there to seek his fortune in the silver mines. "The West is a land of opportunity," he wrote. "Why don't you come out here?" This seemed a good idea, so Milton packed up and went to Denver, where his father was staying. By the time he arrived, however, hard times had hit the mining business. Men were walking the streets looking for jobs, and Milton joined them. He lived with his father for a short time, but soon Henry Hershey was ready to move on again.

Milton found a job at last—in his own line. He became assistant to a Denver candy manufacturer and was pleasantly surprised by the fine quality of the company's products.

SOMERSET COUNTY LIBRARY
SOMERSET, PA. 15501

"Why are your caramels so good?" he asked.

"They are made with fresh milk," his employer said proudly. "That's why they stay sweet and chewy for so long."

I'll remember that, Milton thought.

As time passed, Milton knew he couldn't be happy until he had his own business again. He saved a few hundred dollars, then went to New York City and opened a candy shop. He worked hard, but again found that he could not meet his expenses, nor pay back money he had borrowed to buy new equipment. His business was declared bankrupt, and the sheriff came to close it. Most of the candy-making equipment was taken to satisfy the claims against him. This was humiliating, but Milton worried more because his creditors received only forty cents for every dollar he had borrowed from them. "I'll be back," he told them, "and I'll pay the remaining sixty cents—just as soon as I can."

They laughed at him. Who would expect a bankrupt to be able to pay back—ever —his full debt?

Mrs. Hershey and Aunt Mattie, who had come to help, returned again to Lancaster, and so did Harry Lebkicher. Milton stayed in New York, working as a laborer. Then one day while he was at work, a thief broke into his bedroom and stole everything except the clothes on his back and the money in his pocket. He had just enough to buy a one-way ticket to Lancaster.

During the trip, many thoughts kept going through Milton's mind. After two failures, other young men might have been discouraged and ready to try some other line of work. Not Milton. Candy making was still his business, and he was sure there must be a way to succeed. His two failures had taught him some things he needed to know.

"The secret is specialization," he told himself. "I must concentrate on one product—one kind of candy. And I think I know what it will be—caramels!"

He remembered Denver and the secret of making caramels with fresh milk. Getting fresh milk would be no problem in Lancaster, which was surrounded by dairy farms. Besides, both Aunt Mattie and Harry Lebkicher had always said that Lancaster was the place for him. Maybe they were right. He would ask his uncles to help him start again.

When he arrived in Lancaster, Milton

Devoted Aunt Mattie Snavely helped her nephew Milton with encouragement, money, and hard work.

walked to his Uncle Abraham's farm, several miles from the city. He received a very cool reception and was not even asked inside. Uncle Abraham shook his head as Milton talked about his new plan —to start a caramel business in Lancaster.

"You failed in Philadelphia, and again in New York," his uncle said. "It is time you gave up the candy business, Milton."

"I'm sure I'll make a go of it next time. Caramels—"

"No more money from us," Uncle Abraham said, speaking for himself and Uncle Benjamin, who nodded in agreement.

Milton tramped back to Lancaster to the tiny house his mother and his Aunt Mattie shared. He saw at once there was no room for him, so he left, assuring them that he had a place to stay. Walking aimlessly through the streets, Milton grew more discouraged with each step. He began to think bitterly about his foolishness in coming "home."

Then he remembered Harry Lebkicher. Harry, a bachelor, lived by himself near the Lancaster lumberyard, where he was now working at his old job. Milton walked there and knocked on Harry's door.

Harry's face peered out, and slowly a big smile spread across it. He opened the door and thrust out his hand. "Milton! You're just in time for supper!"

Later Harry told Milton to stay as long as he wished. He also paid the shipping charges on the remainder of Milton's equipment, which had been sent to Lancaster. "You'll be needing your boilers and kettles again, Milton, so you will. You'll make out in Lancaster. I always told you—"

"I know, Harry, and I'll never forget what you've done. If I ever do succeed in the candy business, you'll always be sure of a good job."

"Well, what are we waiting for?" Harry demanded. "I'm ready!"

4. Caramels: A Million Dollar Business

With Harry's help Milton began again. He rented a room in an old warehouse and started making caramels. Whenever he had a basketful, he went out on the streets and peddled them. Slowly, his business started to grow, but he needed more room. So he moved to a factory where there were several other businesses —a carpet beating company, a piano manufacturer, and a carriage maker's shop.

Milton's mother and his Aunt Mattie came to the factory every day and wrapped and packed the caramels. Milton himself, assisted by Harry, did everything else—made the candy, cleaned the kettles, walked to a warehouse for sugar, tramped miles to the farms for milk.

As soon as he had enough money, Milton bought a pushcart. On his first trip to a rough neighborhood, he was stoned and nearly beaten by a gang of boys and young men. He escaped, thankfully, with little damage to himself or to his pushcart.

For some time the struggle to keep going was hard. Then one day a man walked into the factory and asked for Milton Hershey. "My name is Decies," he said. "I'm a candy importer—on a visit here from England." Milton nodded.

"I've tasted your milk caramels," the man went on. "They are the best I've had in America. I'll sell them in England if you can make them in sufficient quantity."

Milton started to exclaim eagerly, "Of course!" He had realized at once that here was a great opportunity. Almost immediately, though, he realized that he needed machinery for large-scale manufacturing! Nobody he knew would lend him any money. Stubbornly, however, he refused to admit failure. Milton told Mr. Decies he would consider the offer.

Milton decided to try borrowing money from a bank. Aunt Mattie offered her small house on Queen Street as security for a loan. Milton began making the rounds of the Lancaster banks, but one bank after another turned him down.

When Milton walked into the Lancaster

National Bank, he was tired and depressed, and he expected the usual refusal. "I need seven hundred dollars," he told the bank cashier, Mr. Brenneman. He went on to explain his candy business. Something about Milton Hershey must have impressed the bank official, for he said quietly, "All right, we'll make the loan—for ninety days."

Quickly Milton bought all the necessary equipment and soon packed his first big order of caramels for England. However, he could not pay back the money he borrowed in ninety days, so again he talked with Mr. Brenneman. "I must have the note renewed," he said. "Besides, I need another thousand dollars—to buy more equipment."

This time Mr. Brenneman shook his head. Even after he inspected Milton's candy factory, he said, "I'm sure this bank will never loan you the money. Still," he continued, "I personally am willing to take a chance. I'll sign your note myself."

Delighted by such confidence in him, Milton worked hard, making more and more caramels, filling new orders that began to come in from the stores and shops in Lancaster. Time passed quickly, and Milton began to worry about paying his note, which was almost due. Then, just a few days before the deadline, he received a check from England. It was the long-awaited payment for the caramels he had shipped—over $2,000!

"Hooray! We've made it!" Milton shouted, waving the check in the air. Then he rushed out to the bank, so excited that he forgot to take off his white apron.

Specializing in one quality product—caramels—was slowly but surely beginning to pay. Milton was on his way now. The orders increased, and he began to make big plans for expansion. He went to the bank again and boldly asked for $100,000. He was shaking a little but his manner was confident. "My business is growing, and I need to rent the whole factory. My present space is not nearly big enough."

"Our bank just can't do it, Milton," Mr. Brenneman said. "But there are banks in New York City able and willing to make such a loan—for a promising business." He recommended one, and soon Milton received the good news that the New York bank would lend him whatever he needed for expansion. Milton raised his original request for $100,000 to $250,000.

Horse-drawn wagons were loaded with candy
at the Lancaster Caramel Company.

Within a short time he had the money.

Now Milton took over the whole factory. Soon he built additions to it. After the many years of struggle, success seemed to come quickly. In a few years the Lancaster Caramel Company became one of the busiest industries in the city, covering a whole city block and employing two thousand workers. Huge kettles bubbled day and night, wafting delicious odors over the neighborhood. Hershey's "Crystal A" caramels were shipped all over the country and to other parts of the world.

Long before his success was so well assured, however, Milton had made a trip to New York and paid off the debts remaining from his business failure there. Now Milton could enjoy his good fortune. He bought a fine house for himself and his mother and painted it yellow and white. He filled it with lovely things, even though his mother shook her head over his foolishness and warned him, "Someday your money will all go, Milton." She never quite believed that his success would not eventually crumble, as his earlier businesses had. Milton merely smiled at her and continued to adorn his home with the bright, cheerful furnishings he loved. His garden was a spot where birds sang and splashed in the fountain. Only one thing saddened him—Aunt Mattie could not share his good fortune. She had died shortly after the caramel business was well established.

In his thriving new caramel business, nobody worked harder than Milton himself, with the possible exception of Harry Lebkicher. Harry became the bookkeeper of the caramel company and Milton's right-hand man. Milton spent much time experimenting to produce better caramels, inventing new shapes and names for them. At first he was his company's best salesman, for he traveled all over the country selling his product.

One day, on one of his visits to a confectionery shop in Jamestown, New York,

Milton noticed a new saleslady behind the counter. She was very attractive, with a rosy complexion and shining auburn hair. He found himself staring at her.

"May I help you?" she asked with a friendly smile.

"Why—why—I—" Milton stammered as he looked into the young lady's deep blue eyes.

Just then the proprietor of the shop rescued him.

"This is Mr. Hershey, Kitty," he said. "Miss Catherine Sweeney."

On his next visit to Jamestown, Milton asked Miss Sweeney to have dinner with him. She accepted and their friendship began. Soon Milton was thinking of her as "my Kitty," and, when she agreed to marry him, he was the happiest man in the world. They were married one lovely spring day in St. Patrick's Cathedral in New York City, and then Milton took Kitty home to Lancaster, where his friends welcomed her and called her "the most beautiful lady."

After his marriage Milton bought another house for his mother and found a companion to look after her. For his father he bought back and remodeled the old Hershey homestead. Henry Hershey settled down contentedly now that he was too old to "flit." Harry Lebkicher lived there with him.

Like thousands of other Americans, Milton had visited the World's Exposition in Chicago in 1893. On his first day there he saw the exhibit of chocolate-making machinery from Germany. Every day after that, as long as he was at the exposition, Milton returned to see chocolate being

Milton Hershey met his wife Kitty, above, in an upstate New York confectionery shop.

made. Shouting to be heard above the throbbing of the machines, the German technician in charge of the machinery explained the process.

"Beans like these," he said, dumping a sackful of the shiny, brown beans into an opening in one of the machines, "come from pods that grow on cacao trees in warm, moist climates."

Milton shouted back. "From Africa and South America. I know."

The other man nodded. "The beans you see here were fermented and dried before being shipped to us. This machine"—he pointed—"is called the 'conche.' It does many things to the beans, but most important it roasts and presses them to release the 'liquor,' which is the basis of all chocolate products."

There were other machines that cooled and solidified the "liquor" to make cocoa and solid bars of chocolate.

Milton, spellbound, watched it all. When the exposition closed, he purchased the machinery and had it shipped to his factory in Lancaster. At first all he had in mind was making enough chocolate to coat the Hershey caramels and to turn out "novelties" like chocolate cigarettes. Although he hired expert chocolate makers, Milton himself spent long hours learning the difficult art of chocolate making. In the meantime, because his interest in chocolate kept growing, he went to Europe and visited the chocolate factories there. He bought more equipment, some of it the first of its kind to be used in the United States.

Gradually Milton began to expand his chocolate business. He was convinced there was a great future in that field. Sometimes he said, "Caramels are only a fad." Then he would add, thoughtfully, "But chocolate—why, that's a food as well as a confection."

In 1900 he had a chance to sell the caramel business. The American Caramel

Company of Philadelphia bought it for $1,000,000. Hershey kept the chocolate business, however, for his own future expansion.

A million dollars for a caramel factory! Lancaster people just couldn't believe it. Milton himself could hardly believe it. What a long way he had come from the days when he had peddled his candies in a pushcart!

5. Factory in a Cornfield

"Has Milton Hershey retired from business?" some people in Lancaster were asking. Many of Milton's friends thought so. "Why not?" they reasoned. "With a million dollars for his caramel factory!"

Milton had no intention of retiring. He became restless as soon as the caramel business passed out of his hands. Kitty wanted a vacation. "Let's take a trip around the world," she said excitedly. "We'll see all the famous places we've read about."

"A good idea," Milton agreed, and they started off by going south to see Latin America. One rainy day in Mexico City Milton stood looking out of his hotel room window, but he was thinking of the green grass and white barns of the Pennsylvania Dutch country. He started talking then about his favorite subject. "Chocolate making has all kinds of possibilities. Fresh milk, which I used in making caramels, will surely make better chocolate. 'Milk Chocolate' will be the Hershey trademark."

His wife smiled. "Are you really enjoying yourself here, Milton?"

"Well—"

"Let's go back home," Kitty proposed.

Milton's eyes lit up. "Are you sure, Kitty?"

"Yes, I am, because I know your heart

is not in this trip. We'll go back and you can start your chocolate factory. There'll be lots of time later for us to travel."

Sometimes, Milton thought happily, Kitty knew his mind better than he did. He did want a chocolate factory—a new one. He was impatient to get started. He would need more machinery than he had, and more men—skilled men. Still he had a million dollars to put into his new business —and he was willing to stake it all on chocolate.

Back home in Lancaster, Milton plunged at once into plans for his new undertaking. "Making chocolate is not easy," he told Kitty.

"No," Kitty agreed. "But if it were easy to make, chocolate would not be so valuable, nor so expensive." Ever since Milton had told her the history of chocolate, Kitty had been deeply interested in its background. "The Aztecs and Mayans even used cacao beans for money," she said, "and the Spanish conquerors thought that 'chocolate' was the most delicious beverage they ever tasted." Kitty continued, thoughtfully, "I'm glad that chocolate is available to almost everybody now, not just the wealthy."

Milton nodded. "Thanks to machinery like mine. But, Kitty, I'm wondering where to build my new factory. In Lancaster? Philadelphia?"

He didn't say so at first, even to Kitty, but somehow the prospect of city surroundings for a bright new factory did not please him. Why not have it in the country? Milk would be plentiful from the rich dairy farms of the area—the right kind of milk, too, from Holstein cows.

His thoughts kept going back to the country village he had known in boyhood —Derry Church. When he had it settled in his own mind, Kitty was the first to know. She listened to him in amazement, then declared forthrightly, "Milton, you ought to have your head examined!"

He chuckled. "I'm sure that's what my business friends will say, too!" Back in 1900, building a big factory out in the country was unheard of.

"What will you do for workers—and transportation—and houses for your workers?" Harry Lebkicher wanted to know. "Where will you find employees in the middle of a cornfield?"

"I'll be able to get the best in the world in Derry Church! I know those people. As for transportation and houses— I'll build them! I'll build a whole town!"

Harry, "Mother" Hershey, Kitty, all his friends shook their heads. They doubted his judgment. Yet Milton Hershey was the man who had refused to stay down when he had been knocked down—twice. He was the man who built a tiny caramel shop into a million dollar business. He had his mother's common sense and his father's daring, as well as his own streak of stubbornness. He went ahead with his plans.

Milton toured the area of Derry Church. "That's where I want the factory," he told his surveyors. "Streets and houses here—and here. A school, churches, a hospital. A park over there. Lots of land for expansion, and a trolley line from Lancaster. Now what about the water mains?"

The old Hershey homestead became the

center of activity while the factory and town were being built. Nobody enjoyed the bustle and excitement more than Henry Hershey. He followed every step of the plans and was as enthusiastic as Milton. "At last Milton is doing things in a big way," he said with satisfaction.

Work began in 1903 on Milton's dream come true—a factory near rural Derry Church.

Milton had a test plant built next to the homestead, and he started experimenting there—working out new formulas to use in his chocolate products. He tried many different combinations of milk, sugar, and chocolate, and discarded them when they did not turn out right. Different degrees of condensing and heat were tried—until he got just the result he wanted. Then he would call out exultantly, "I've got it!"

By the time the factory was built, in 1904, Milton had what he thought was the best blend of chocolate that could be produced. The great machines, operated by a huge dynamo, began the long, difficult process of changing cacao beans into chocolate bars. Milton put the best man he had in charge of the factory—his former top salesman, Bill Murrie.

"Come and help me celebrate," he told his friends the day the factory opened. So they came, the leading businessmen and many public officials from Lancaster, Lebanon, Hummelstown, Campbelltown, and Hockersville. The new trolley was busy that day. At the last stop Milton Hershey boarded the trolley to welcome his guests, then led them on a tour of his marvelous new chocolate factory. They were almost speechless with admiration. Many of these same men had shaken their heads over the foolishness of building a chocolate factory in a cornfield. Now at dinner they drank toasts to the success of Milton Hershey's dream.

6. The Chocolate Town

Milton enjoyed himself as the chocolate town rose around the factory. He instructed the builders and joked with the bricklayers and plasterers. He gave directions to the architects. He did not want a dreary company town of look-alike houses. "Each house should have a style of its own, and a lawn, and room for a garden."

The houses were comfortable and attractive, built on tree-shaded streets called Trinidad, Java, Granada—as reminders of the chocolate industry. Chocolate Avenue was the wide main thoroughfare, and the center of town was the place where Cocoa Avenue crossed Chocolate. Near here were the stores, the bank, post office, inn, and railroad station. Even the street lights of Hershey carried out the chocolate theme. They were shaped like Hershey kisses!

Milton built a big house for Kitty and himself and furnished it with the beautiful things they had brought back from their travels. Milton and Kitty had traveled abroad many times since their marriage. They had seen the beauty spots of Europe and the Orient, as well as all the fashionable places of America. They could live anywhere they chose. Yet Kitty smiled when Milton said so. "Do you suppose you could be happy anywhere but in your chocolate town?" she asked.

Their home, called "High Point," stood on a hill across the creek from the factory. Here the Hersheys were close enough to see the factory chimney stacks through the trees and smell the chocolate fragrance that came wafting out from those chimneys at regular intervals. Jokingly, the workers of Hershey called that smell "the chocolate stink." However, to Milton —and to Kitty, too—it was the loveliest aroma in the world.

Next came a park for the people of Hershey. Located behind the factory, the park contained everything for wholesome recreation—amusements, a zoo, a golf course, a football field, a dancing pavilion, and an outdoor theater.

Although Henry Hershey died before the town was completed, Milton's mother, with her companion, came to live in the

Children who visit the town of Hershey enjoy seeing the animals in the zoo and going on rides in the park.

chocolate town in a new house Milton built for her. On one of his daily visits she said, "Give me some work to do, Milton. 'Idleness is the devil's workbench.' "

He nodded. "I'll send you some work, Mother."

Every day from then on, Mrs. Hershey spent her mornings wrapping silver paper around Hershey kisses that were brought to her from the factory. She kept on helping her son until she died at 84. One of her last pieces of advice to Milton was, "Don't let your money spoil you."

After his mother's death Milton gave money in her name to the Mennonite Church of Lancaster for an old people's home.

7. The School for Boys

Milton Hershey's chocolate factory became one of the great businesses in the country. The town of Hershey was prosperous because it was built on the manufacturing of chocolate, which was in ever-increasing demand by the American people. Steadily and surely the money came in. Milton poured most of it back into the factory and the town—building additions and adding the latest machinery —but even so, he and his wife had more money than they could ever spend. Basically their tastes were simple, and they both felt they wanted to do something worthwhile with their riches.

The Hersheys were fond of children, but they had none of their own. One day, as they discussed the best way to use their money, Kitty suddenly clapped her hands. "Let's start a home for children who have no one to provide for them."

"A home for orphan boys," Milton said slowly. "And a school. Yes, I think that's the best thing we could do. Boys have to learn a trade—as I did—and find a job. If they have no parents to help them, they may never get their chance."

Kitty's eyes glowed. "Build the school nearby, Milton, so that we can visit often." She added, a little wistfully, "Maybe they will visit us." Kitty's health was slowly failing. Most of the traveling she did now with Milton was in search of doctors who

might cure her. Milton took her to every specialist he could find.

Milton agreed on the school's location and soon had plans drawn up for the Hershey Industrial School, as it was known at first. The sturdy old homestead provided living quarters for the first boys who came—two small brothers whose father had died, leaving the family penniless. Other orphan boys, many of them

from the cities and towns near Hershey,
followed. The boys grew up in the healthy
country atmosphere that Milton Hershey
wanted for them—the kind he had known
in childhood. On the homestead farm they
learned how to plant crops and milk cows,
take care of chickens and horses, use
machinery, build, and repair. Fun and play
were also part of their schedule—skating
in winter and swimming in summer. There

81

were kind people in charge and good wholesome food. As time passed, more boys came to Milton Hershey's school.

Milton visited the school often, sad that Kitty was not well enough to accompany him. At his invitation the boys took turns going to the mansion for Sunday dinner. Their visits always made Kitty feel better.

Although Milton Hershey started the school with the idea of teaching boys a useful trade, as time went on the scope of the school broadened. High school and college preparation were included for those boys who were able and interested. From the handful who came first, the school grew to over a thousand boys.

Kitty's illness finally took her life in 1915. Milton, in his grief, determined to devote his fortune to the school she had helped him start.

8. Hershey, U.S.A.

After Kitty's death Milton traveled more
than ever. New scenes and people helped
to ease his heartache. He especially loved
Cuba and spent a great deal of time there.
He bought sugarcane fields and built a
town called Central Hershey, where the
chief industry was refining sugar for the
Hershey chocolate factory.

Then a day came, in 1920, when Milton
recalled what his mother had often warned
him about his money. "It will all go."

Business seemed to be so good that the Hershey Chocolate Company needed even more sugar than it could get from Cuba. However, prices were skyrocketing. Milton bought too much at top prices. Then the demand for his products dropped, and he had to sell them at a great loss. He lost several million dollars and had to ask a bank for a loan. He received the money, but the bank took a mortgage on his property and sent a manager to run the business.

Milton told the workers of Hershey, "We'll come back—stronger than ever." He was determined not to be beaten. Leading the way by working long, hard hours, he found new outlets for Hershey's chocolate—at home and abroad. He cut down expenses and tightened up schedules. After only one year the company was again making a profit, and the bank's manager left.

Milton breathed a sigh of relief. He had pulled through. Now, however, he decided that his company was too big to be run by one man, even though he was the man. He reorganized the business, making three companies instead of one. One company would take care of the chocolate business, another the sugar interests in Cuba, and the third the business affairs of the town of Hershey. All three were controlled by the Hershey Trust Company for the benefit of the Milton Hershey School.

In the 1930s came the Great Depression. Money was scarce, men lost their jobs, thousands of people all over the country lined up at free soup kitchens or tried to sell apples on street corners.

Milton Hershey and his closest associates met to discuss ways to get safely through the depression. Everyone was worried except Milton Hershey himself. He had been through too many ups and downs in business to fear anything now. Besides he had a plan to keep Hershey going. "I think we should start to build," he said calmly. "The men in the town must have work, and we must provide it or feed them."

His friends did not agree. "This is no time to build!" they said. "Suppose the market for chocolate disappears? What will you use for capital?"

"We'll cross that bridge later—if necessary," Milton replied. He set his men to work completing the beautiful Community Building on Chocolate Avenue that housed a theater, a gymnasium, a swimming pool,

and a library. Then he made plans for a resort hotel on the summit of Patt's Hill, overlooking the town. Long ago, when he and Kitty had stayed in the great Heliopolis Hotel in Cairo, which she had enjoyed, she'd said, "Let's build a hotel like this in Hershey, Milton." He agreed.

Again people told Milton he was extravagant as well as foolish to put so much money into a hotel! He smiled and said, "Other men have yachts to play with. The hotel is my yacht." When the Hershey Hotel was finished, it did not resemble just the Heliopolis Hotel. Instead it combined the features of many lovely hotels the Hersheys had visited in their travels.

Hershey's building program during the depression years included the huge junior-senior high school that became part of the Milton Hershey School and a new air-conditioned office building. The sports arena and the stadium made the town of Hershey famous for ice hockey and football. Facilities for other sports, from tennis to golf, were provided in Hershey.

When the depression came to an end, Milton Hershey said with great satisfaction, "No man in Hershey lost his job and no salaries were cut."

Then in 1937 labor troubles struck Hershey. Union organizers came to the town and led the workers on a strike for better hours and wages. The factory was closed for the first time, while pickets marched up and down. The strike ended quickly, however, when the farmers of the area took matters into their own hands. They did not intend to stand by and see millions of gallons of their precious milk being spoiled! Enraged, they armed

themselves with clubs, marched on the union men, and drove them from the factory and out of town. Later, however, Milton Hershey brought representatives of the workers and the company together and helped them to settle their differences. An employees' union was recognized and peace returned to Hershey.

Milton Hershey never lost his interest in experimenting and in trying new things. He was 84 when the United States entered World War II. Soon afterward the government asked him to fill a special order. The army wanted a chocolate bar for a soldier to carry as food—chocolate that would not melt in his pocket, and that would keep him alive in an emergency when no other food was available.

Milton Hershey welcomed the challenge. He made a new thick chocolate bar called

"Field Ration D." This was so successful that the army kept increasing its orders until the factory at Hershey was turning out 500,000 bars a day. Overseas, soldiers everywhere used his "Field Ration D" for barter as well as for food.

For this service the United States government gave the company a special achievement award and the Army-Navy E Flag for excellence. The flag flew proudly over the chocolate factory. Milton was happy because he could serve his country.

Even as he neared the end of his days, he still looked ahead. "Everything I built will go on," he told visitors to "High Point." "The factory will continue to support the town." He smiled when he added, "The chocolate fragrance will keep on pouring from the smokestacks."

Long after Milton Hershey's death in

1945 at the age of 88, visitors from every part of the world still come to Hershey. They come to see the well-ordered town and its beautiful buildings. They walk through gardens lovely at all seasons of the year, and of course tour the famous chocolate factory. Everything in Hershey is a memorial to the energy and courage of a little Pennsylvania Dutch boy who became the world's chocolate king— Hershey Park, the Rose Gardens, the Sports Arena, Hotel Hershey, the Hershey Museum. The greatest monument of all, the one closest to his heart, is the school he founded and endowed with his fortune. The Milton Hershey School has already prepared thousands of young Americans to be useful citizens. This it will continue to do, even as it changes to meet the needs of a changing world.

Index